Shoe
Coloring Book
For Adults

30 Hand Drawn Paisley and Henna Ladies Shoe Fashion Coloring Pages

By
Louise Ford

ISBN-13: 978-1540628176
ISBN-10: 1540628175

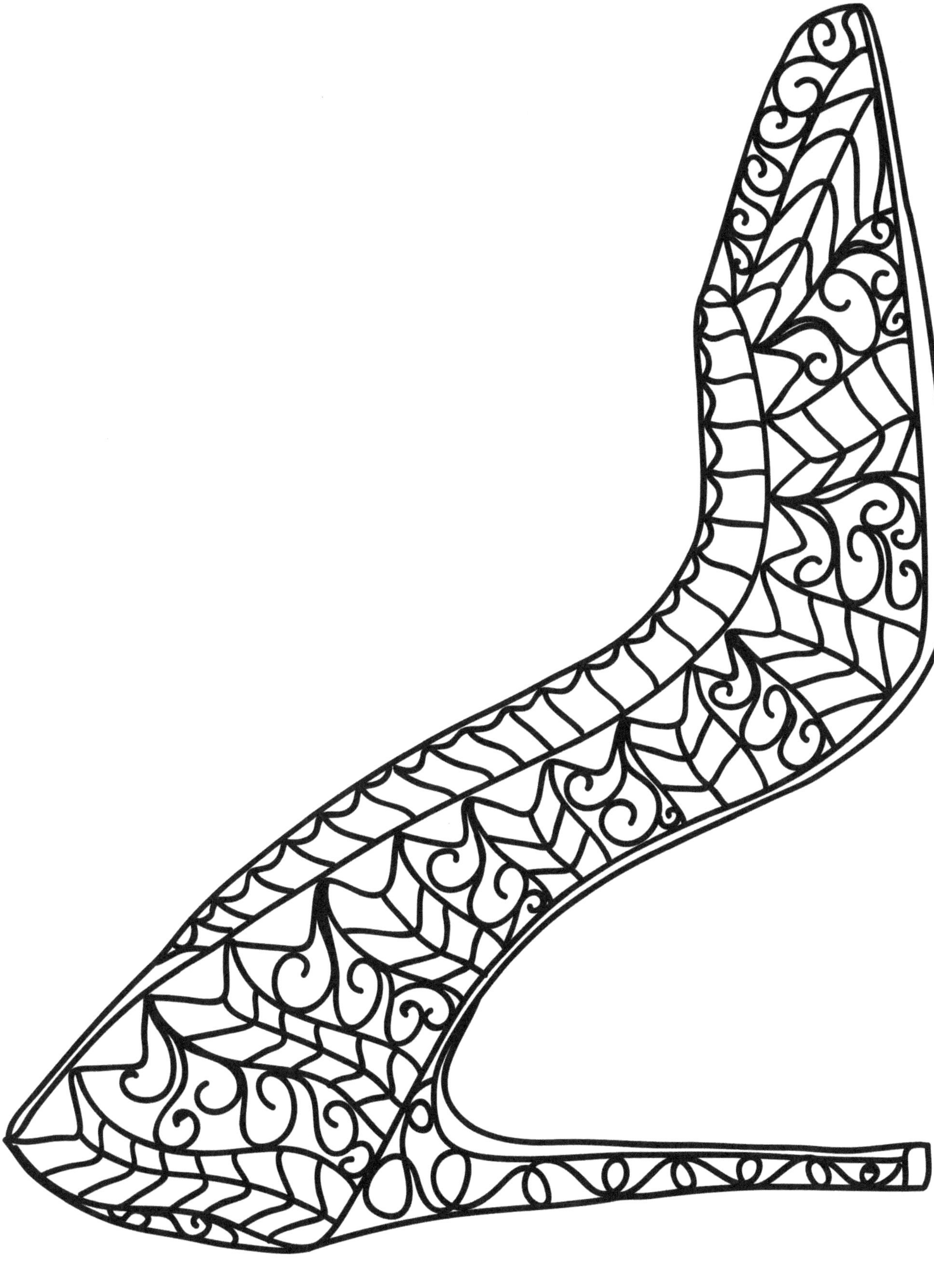

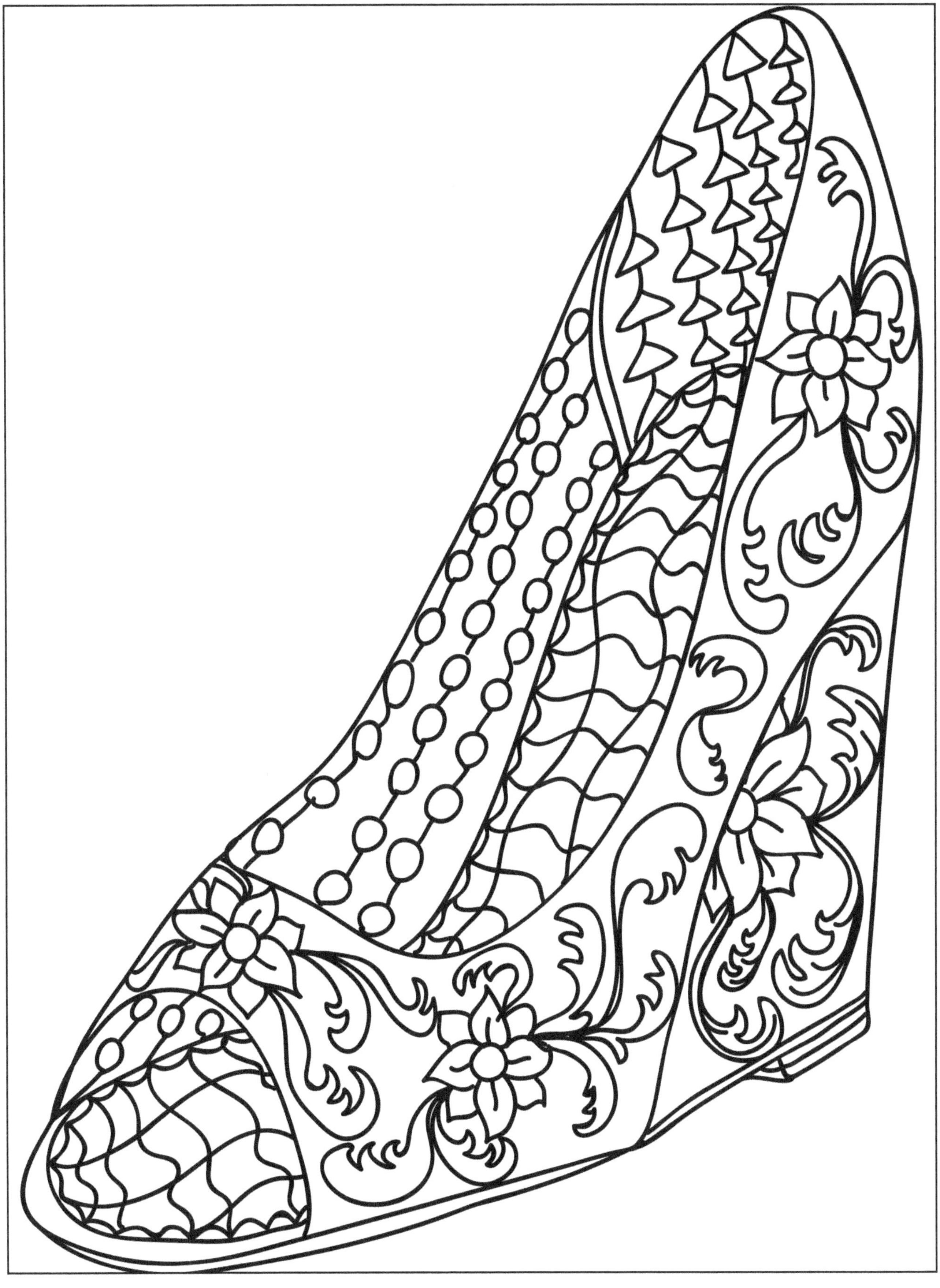

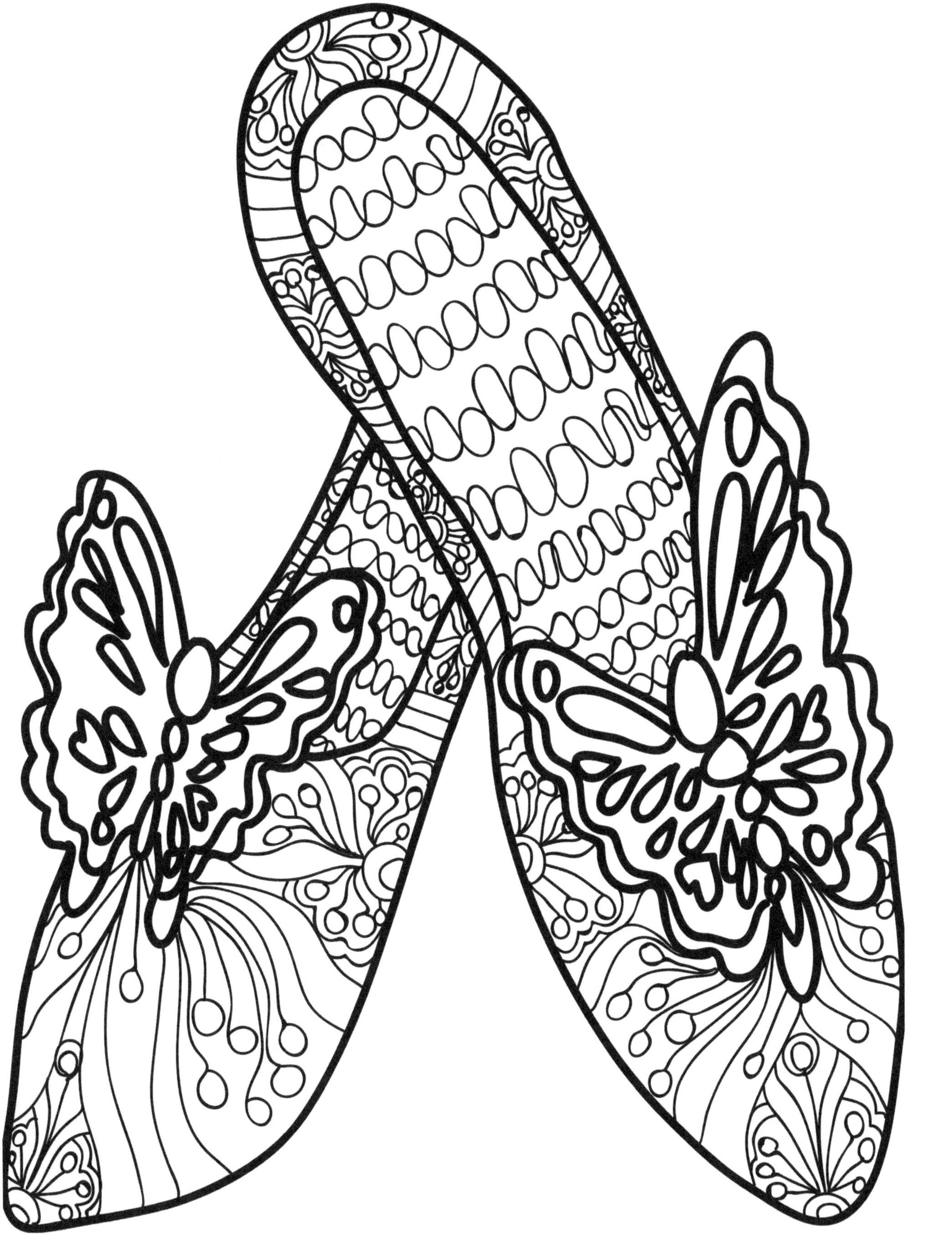

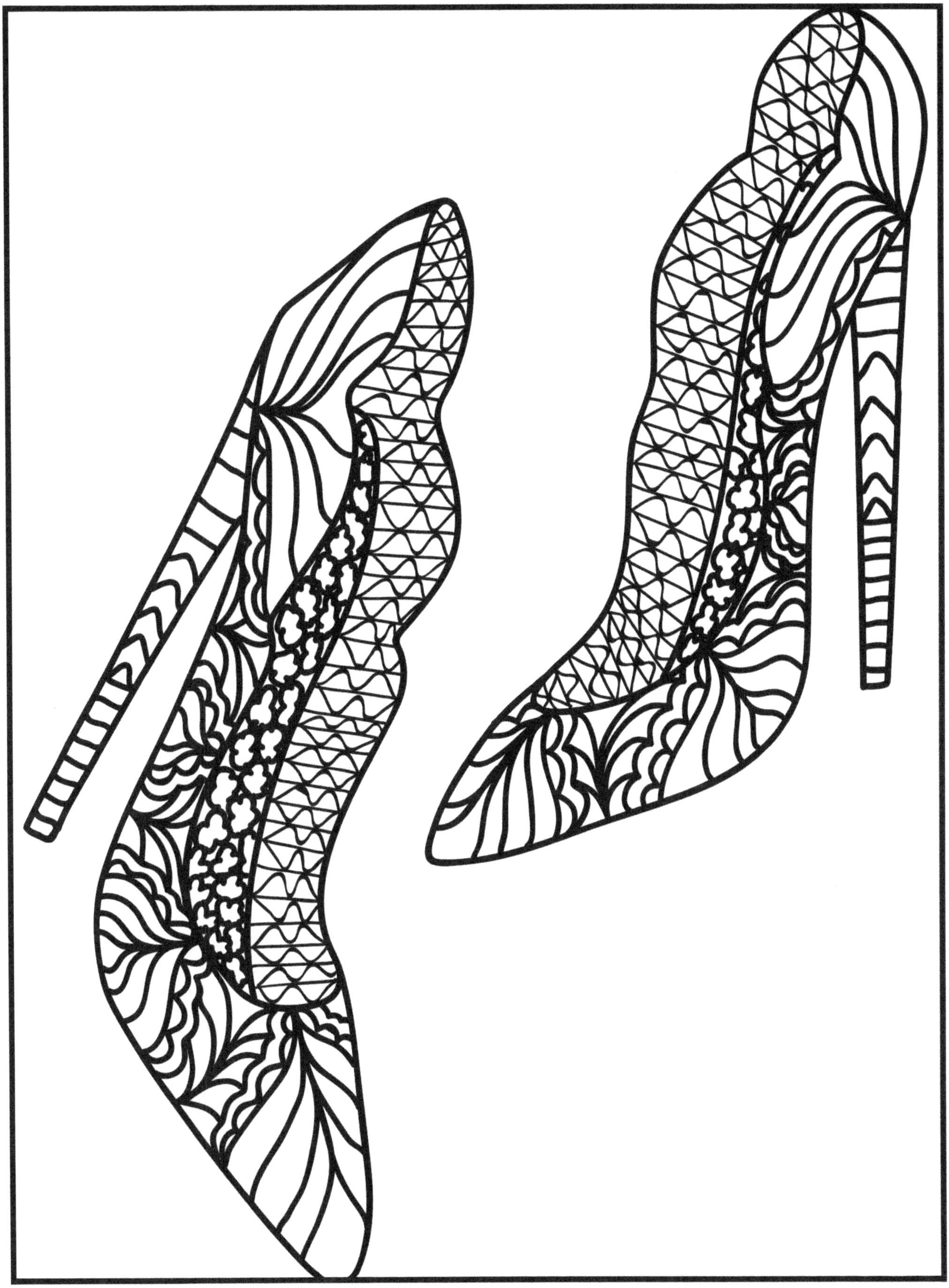

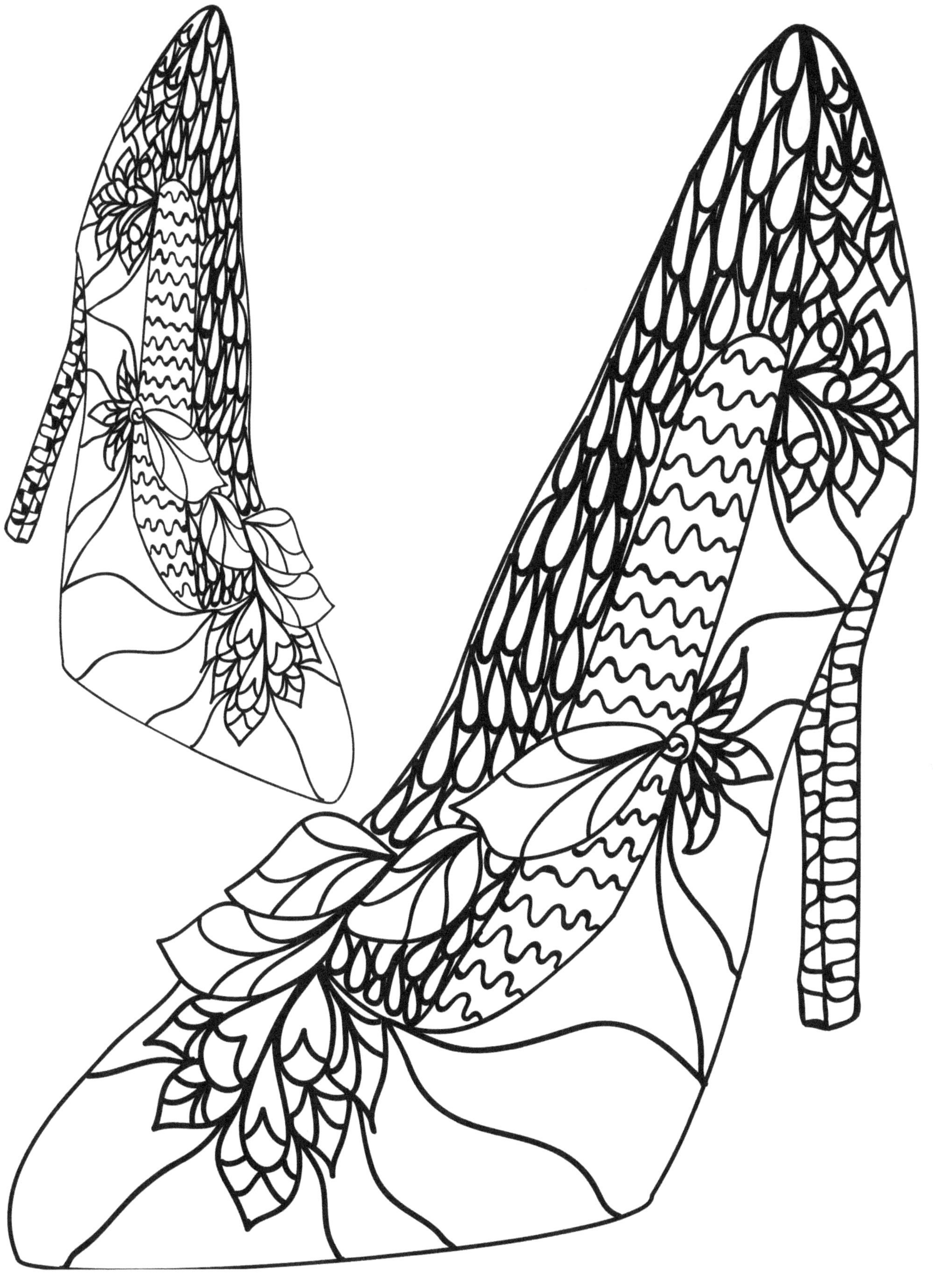

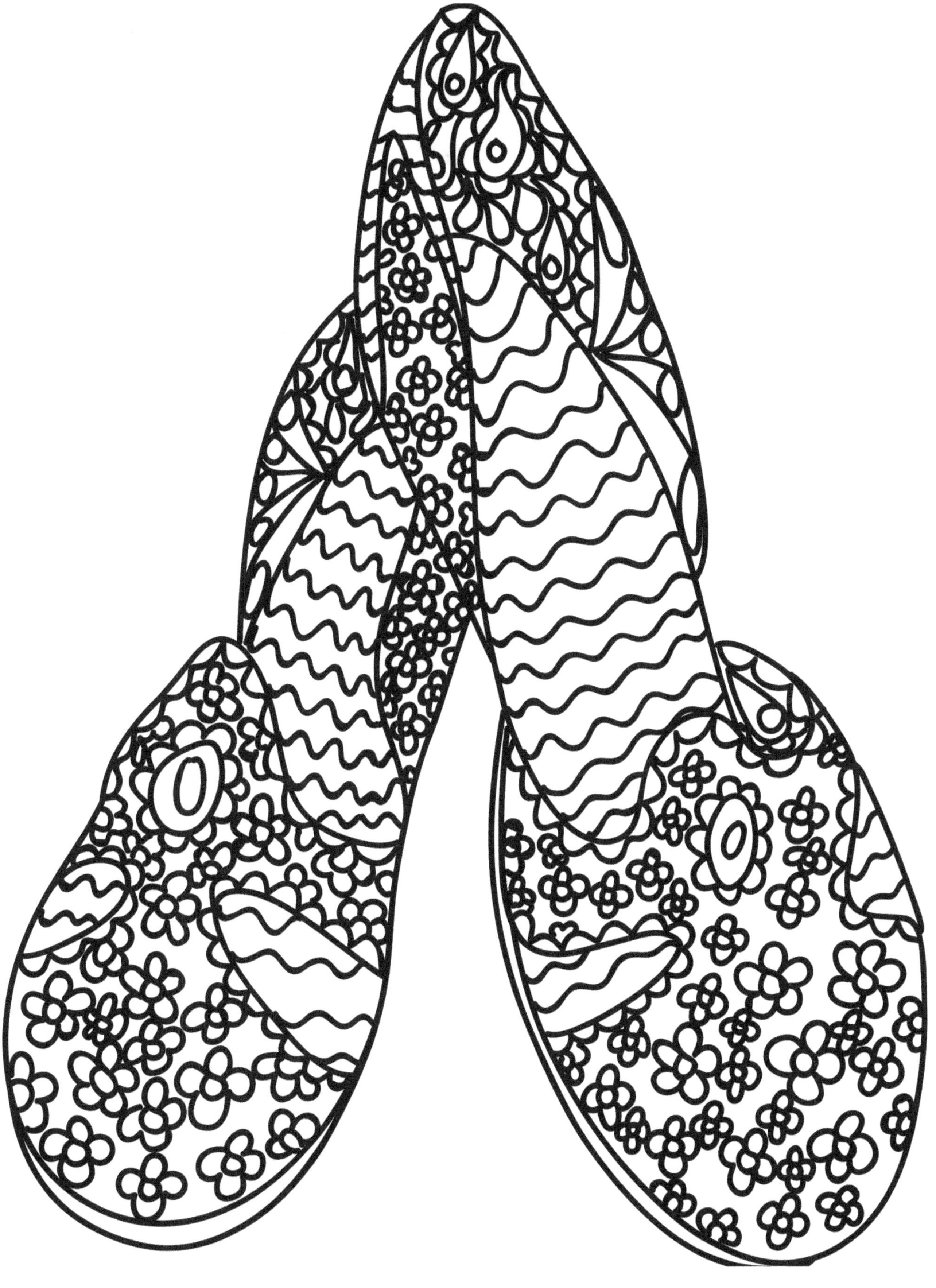

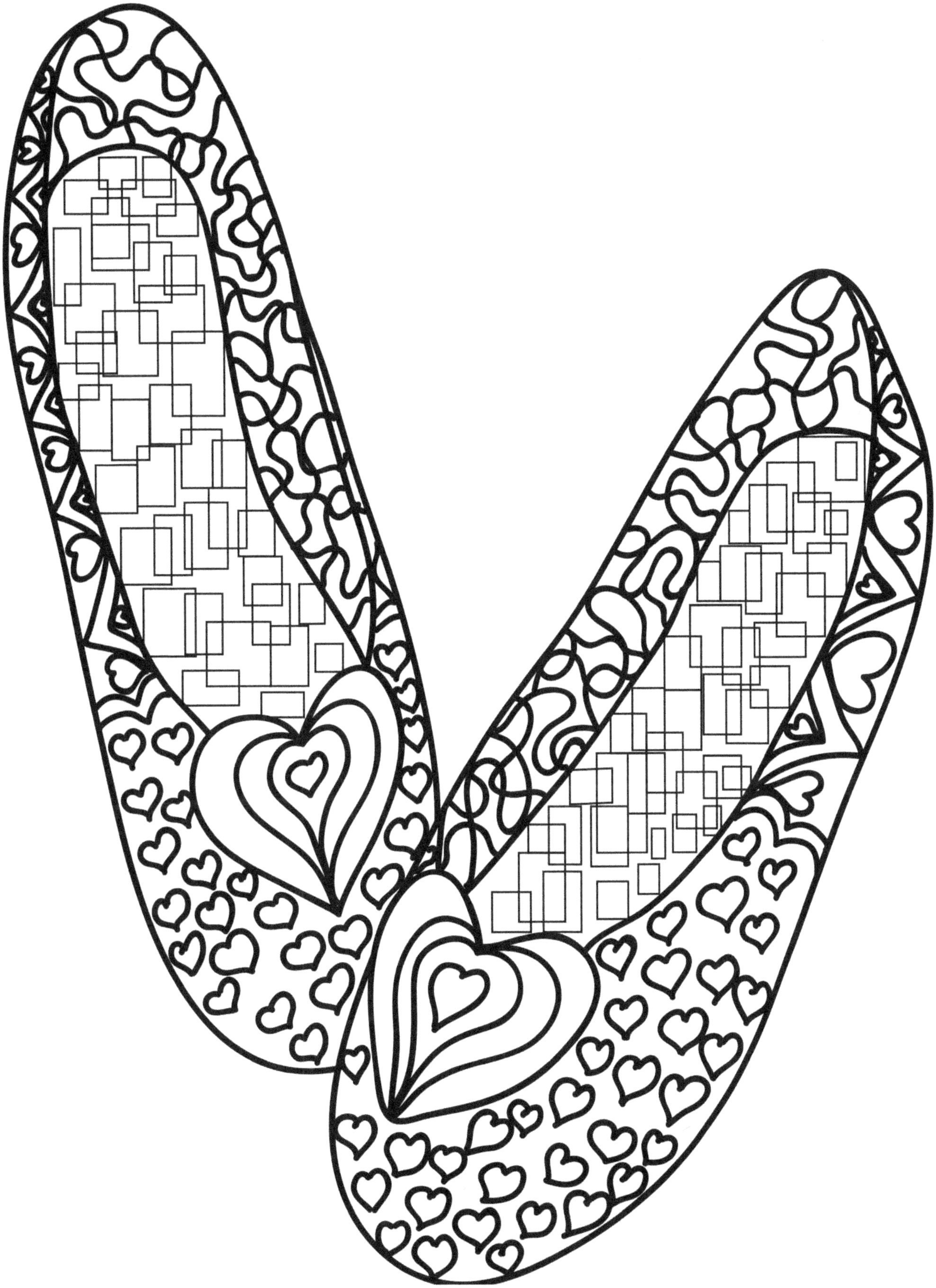

www.ingramcontent.com/pod-product-compliance
Lightning Source LLC
Chambersburg PA
CBHW081859280526
45789CB00007B/2764
9781540628176